MW00571373

Sporting Record-Breakers

LAGOON BOOKS

Series Editor: Heather Dickson

Research: Danielle Williams, Henrietta McMicking,
Matthew Hirtes, Russell Walton, Sheila Harding

Additional contributors: Peter Kirkham,
Ann Marangos, Gaby Wirminghaus

Illustrations: Andrew Sheerin

Page design and layout: Linley Clode

Cover design: Gary Inwood Studios

Published by:
LAGOON BOOKS
PO BOX 311, KT2 5QW, UK

ISBN: 1899712755

© LAGOON BOOKS, 1999

Lagoon Books is a trade mark of
Lagoon Trading Company Limited. All rights reserved.

Printed in Singapore

Sporting
Record-Breakers

LAGOON
BOOKS

Other titles available from Lagoon Books:

Introduction

At last – a follow-up to the enormously popular Sports Trivia Quiz!

Although similar in style – with every imaginable type of question on just about every sport – Sporting Record-Breakers has the added attraction of concentrating on those who are the very best in their fields. Sportsmen who made it into the record book by becoming the first-ever holder of a title or by achieving a new fastest speed. Teams that have won the most titles and countries that have scooped the most medals in the Summer and Winter Olympics through the years.

The book can either be enjoyed alone or, for those with a competitive streak, played as a sports quiz by a group.

TO PLAY: split players into two teams. Each team should nominate one player to read the questions. Team 1 should choose a page in the book and read the questions on that page to Team 2. Team 2 should then choose another page and read the questions on that page to Team 1.

TO SCORE: if the question has only one answer, score 8 points. If the question has eight separate answers, score 1 point for each answer you get correct.

At the end of the game count how many points each team has scored – the team with the highest score is the winner!

What is the longest...?

A) Golf hole in the world

B) Winning margin in a Classic horse race

C) Grand slam tennis match

D) Olympic career

E) Cricket test match

F) Baseball throw

G) Boxing match

H) Ski jump

1

Guess the sporting record-breaker

A) This American was born Walker Smith

B) He entered his first competition on a borrowed licence, and that was how he got his name

C) He won his first world title in 1946

D) He was a Golden Gloves featherweight and lightweight champion

E) He won the world middleweight title on five separate occasions

F) He announced his retirement in 1952, but came back and regained his title two years later

G) The NBA deprived him of his title in 1959 because he had taken too long to defend it, but it was still recognised by the NYAC

H) He was finally defeated in 1960 by Paul Pender

2

What is the greatest speed ever achieved by...?

A) A bicycle

B) A skier

C) A sailing boat

D) A horse

E) A greyhound

F) A skater

G) A runner

H) A swimmer

3

The Olympics

A) Which country has hosted the Olympics the most times?

B) Which athlete has won the most Olympic medals?

C) In which Olympics did the most athletes participate?

D) Who is the only person to win a gold medal at the Summer and Winter Olympics?

E) Who was the oldest Olympic medallist?

F) Which Olympian has competed in the most Games?

G) Who is the youngest gold medallist?

H) Who has won the most gold medals in one Games?

4

Guess the year that all the following occurred

A) Dan O'Brien of the USA set new world and American records for the decathlon

B) Keirin Perkins of Australia set a world record by swimming the 1,500m freestyle in 14 minutes 43.48 seconds

C) Jan Zelezny joined the history makers by throwing the javelin a world record distance of 294ft 2in

D) Kevin Young of the USA ran the 400m hurdles in 46.28 seconds, to smash the world record

E) Yevgeny Sadovyi of the (Soviet) Unified Team broke world and Olympic records in this year with the 200m and 400m freestyle respectively

F) Quincy Watts ran the 400m in an Olympic record-breaking time of 43.50 seconds

G) South Korea went home victorious this year by taking Olympic gold for the single 1,000m short-track speedskating event, and for the 4 x 1,250m team events

H) The American sprint team won the 4 x 100m in a world record time of just 37.40 seconds

5

What is the highest...?

A) Number of international appearances made by a soccer player

B) Attendance at a tennis match

C) Number of tries scored by a single player in a Rugby Union match

D) Number of goals scored in a soccer match by a single player

E) Score in an international basketball game

F) Average score in Tenpin Bowling World Championship doubles

G) Speed reached at the end of a 440-yard run (Drag racing)

H) Score in an international handball match

6

Soccer World Cup

A) Which country has won the Championship the most times?

B) Which player has made the most individual appearances in the World Cup?

C) Who is the oldest player to have taken part in the competition?

D) Name the only country to have participated in all 16 World Cup Finals

E) Who is the only soccer player to score a hat-trick in a World Cup Final?

F) Which country has scored the most goals during a single tournament?

G) Which player has been in three World Cup winning teams?

H) What is the most goals a team has scored in a single World Cup game?

Guess the sporting record-breaker

A) He won four gold medals at the 1984 Olympics

B) He has an awesome total of nine Olympic golds

C) His mother was a talented hurdler, and his sister gained fame before him

D) His first Olympic selection didn't get him to the Games because his country boycotted Moscow

E) He was a part of the relay team that took the only world record of the 1984 Olympics

F) He won the 1991 World Championship 100m in 9.86 seconds

G) He held the world long jump record for 10 years, and had 65 victories

H) He finished second, but won gold, in the 1988 Olympics when the victor tested positive for steroids

8

Round the world

A) Who was the first person to circumnavigate the earth?

B) Which yachtsman was the first to sail solo round the world?

C) What is the fastest time round the world in a boat?

D) Who was the first female sailor to scoop the solo non-stop record?

E) By what means did Ron Bauer and John Williams circumnavigate the world in 17 days, 16 hours, 14 minutes?

F) Who was the first man to walk round the world?

G) What is the fastest trip round the world on scheduled flights?

H) Which balloonist has set a record for the longest distance completed in his attempt to fly round the world?

9

Who was the first...?

A) Cricketer to take 100 wickets and score 1,000 runs in a single season

B) Boxer to win titles in more than two weights

C) Black winner of a grand slam tennis title

D) Athlete to clear 100 metres with the javelin

E) Holder of the World Motor Racing Champion title

F) To ride 1,000 National Hunt winners

G) Darts player to score 501 in nine darts

H) Female tennis player to win £1 million in prize money

10

The US Masters

A) Who won the Masters for a sixth time in 1986?

B) Who set the record in 1997 for winning by the greatest margin, a record 12 strokes?

C) Who holds the record for making the most cuts in the Masters?

D) Who, in 1955, became a runner-up for a record-breaking fourth time?

E) Who remains the oldest first time winner in the history of the Masters?

F) Who set a dubious record in 1956 when he shot a score of 95, the highest ever in the competition?

G) Who set a record in 1986 for the 10 birdies he shot in one round, for a score of 63?

H) Who staged a record nine stroke comeback in the final round to clinch the 1956 Masters title?

11

Super Bowl

A) Which team has won the most titles?

B) Who is the only individual player to have won five times?

C) Which Super Bowl game has attracted the greatest television audience?

D) Who has won the Most Valuable Player award the most times?

E) What is the highest team score?

F) Which coach has recorded the most wins?

G) Which Super Bowl game has attracted the largest crowd?

H) Which game has set the record for the highest aggregate score?

12

Guess the country

A) This country boasts the Olympic Rugby champions! They were the winners when the game was dropped from the Olympics in 1924

B) It holds a record for being in the top three medal-winning countries in the Olympics, failing only once, in 1980

C) It took the Admiral's Cup yachting trophy away from Britain for the first time in 1961

D) This country's representatives far outstrip any rivals in women's tennis grand slam singles titles

E) Its sportsmen have the Olympic medals for the 200m and 400m sprints and relays

F) It hosts the youngest of the grand slam golfing tournaments

G) In tennis, 1971 was the first time in 16 years that its Opens tennis tournament was won by locals, making Stan Smith and Billy Jean King sporting heroes

H) It hosted the 1996 Olympic Games

Stadiums around the world

A) Where is the world's most expensive stadium?

B) Which stadium has the greatest capacity for spectators?

C) Which football match attracted a record crowd at Wembley Stadium?

D) Where is the largest soccer stadium in the world?

E) Where is the Mile-High Stadium?

F) Which is the largest National Football League stadium?

G) Where is the largest covered stadium?

H) The largest cricket ground in the world has a capacity of 130,000. Where is it?

14

How long did the following record-breakers retain their records?

A) Joe Louis – World Heavyweight Boxing Champion

B) Jesse Owens – Long jump

C) Hanif Mohamed – 499 score in a single cricket innings

D) Roger Maris – Highest Major League home runs in a season

E) Jacques Edmund Barre – Real Tennis Champion

F) Gisela Mauermayer – Women's discus

G) Mahmoud – Fastest Derby

H) Bob Beamon – Long jump

15

Guess the sporting record-breaker

A) The first main race he won was in Formula Konig at Hockenheim in April 1988

B) He has often been compared to Ayrton Senna in personality and drive

C) He was ranked number 1 in 1996 for "Men of the Year – Personalities who Shape Motorsport"

D) He won the 1994 and 1995 World Championship

E) By the end of the 1998 season, he had recorded 33 wins, 65 podium finishes, and 19 pole positions

F) He equalled Nigel Mansell's 1992 record of nine wins in a season in 1995

G) He was described in 1994 by Nigel Roebuck as "... having a degree of talent seen only once or twice in a generation"

H) He has a famous brother called Ralf

Which country...?

A) Won the bronze, silver and gold medals in the women's 800 metres at the Moscow Olympics

B) Has won the most medals in Olympic bobsleighing

C) Was the first to beat the USA in the America's Cup

D) Has scored the most points in an International Rugby Union match

E) Defeated the USA's basketball team for the first time in the Olympic 1972 Final

F) Has won the most Olympic water polo titles

G) Has retained the Olympic Rugby Union title since 1924

H) Has won the most Fly-Fishing World Championship team titles

17

Guess the year that all the following occurred

A) Jackie Joyner-Kersee pounced on the Olympic record with a distance of 24ft 3.25in in the women's long jump

B) A new Olympic 3,000m steeplechase record was set by Julius Karioki with a time of 8 minutes 5.51 seconds

C) Paula Ivan of Romania left with not only an Olympic gold for her 1,500m run in this year, but took the Olympic record too

D) Florence Griffith-Joyner became the fastest woman in the world by running the 100m in an unbelievable 10.49 seconds

E) Kristin Otto took home more Olympic medals than anybody else in this year, and they were all gold! She won all six swimming events that she competed in

F) In speedskating, Tomas Gustafson showed his style by setting world records in both the 5,000m and 10,000m

G) Yvonne Van Gonnip of the Netherlands cleared the field in ladies' speedskating, when she set an Olympic record for the 1,500m, and world records for both the 3,000m and 5,000m

H) Jackie Joyner-Kersee set the Olympic and world women's records in the heptathlon

18

Who was the youngest to...?

A) Win a World Boxing Championship

B) Win a men's tennis grand slam tournament

C) Play in the NBA

D) Score a hole-in-one in golf

E) Win a F1 Grand Prix World Championship

F) Win a canoe gold at the Olympics

G) Become a professional World Snooker Champion

H) Compete as a gymnast in an international competition

19

Who holds the world record for the following events?

A) 100 metres

B) 1 mile

C) 110-metre hurdles

D) High jump

E) Triple jump

F) Javelin

G) Discus

H) Shot

20

Which sport do the following record-holders play?

A) Shaun Pollock – South Africa

B) Vivien Jones – Wales

C) Greg Louganis – United States

D) Paul Litjens – The Netherlands

E) Ingrid Christiansen – Norway

F) Miguel Indurain – Spain

G) Inna Valeryevna – USSR

H) Ritchie Gardner – UK

On record, what is the fastest...?

A) Baseball pitch

B) Try in an international Rugby Union game

C) F1 Grand Prix lap

D) 5,000 metres (Athletics)

E) Tennis serve

F) Cricket ball bowled

G) 10-kilometre Biathlon in the Winter Olympic Games

H) Women's 20-kilometre walk

22

Guess the sporting record-breaker

A) This left-handed player hails from America

B) He won a record eight matches at Wimbledon in 1977, to take him from the qualifying competition to the semi-finals without a defeat

C) He had his first grand slam success in 1977 paired with Mary Carillo in the French Open

D) He won the US Singles four times

E) He has won nine doubles grand slam titles

F) He holds a record of seven consecutive Masters wins paired with Peter Fleming

G) He has won the Wimbledon Singles three times

H) He is most famous for the verbal abuse he aimed at court officials for their perceived inadequacies while he was playing

23

What do the following record-breakers have in common?

A) John Lee Richmond – Baseball

B) Hans Eugster – Gymnastics

C) Jayne Torville and Christopher Dean – Figure Skating

D) EJ Murt O'Donoghue - Snooker

E) Michael Holman Finneran – Diving

F) Nadia Comaneci – Gymnastics

G) Frankie Dettori – Horse-racing

H) Marina Lobach – Rhythmic Sportive Gymnastics

Snooker

A) Who won the World Professional Championship a record 15 times?

B) Who is the youngest player to win a World Professional title?

C) In 1983 Cliff Thorburn became the first person to do what in a World Professional Championship tournament?

D) Who holds the record for most tons by one player in a tournament, by making an incredible 14 centuries during the 1998 World Championship?

E) Which six-time world champion, nicknamed "The Nugget", was the first to make three consecutive century breaks in a major tournament?

F) Who holds the record for the fastest maximum ever made?

G) Which world champion had been in the top 16 world rankings for 11 consecutive seasons by the 1998/99 season?

H) Who won "Achievement of the Year" in 1995 for becoming the first teenager to win three world ranking tournaments, namely the Grand Prix, the International Open, and the British Open?

Animal Magic

A) What is the highest price paid for a racehorse?

B) What greyhound has had the most career wins?

C) What is the highest a horse has jumped on record?

D) What is the greatest distance completed by a pigeon in a competitive race?

E) In 1985-86 which British greyhound eclipsed Joe Dump's record of 31 consecutive wins?

F) What is the biggest fish ever caught on a rod?

G) Name the world's most successful racehorse ever

H) Name the greyhound with the most wins in a year

26

In which racket sports do the following hold records?

A) Manuel de Souza-Girao – Spain

B) Park Joo-Bay – South Korea

C) Egan Inoue – USA

D) Pierre Etchebaster – France

E) John Donald Budge – USA

F) Angelica Rozeaun – Romania

G) David Dumner Milford and John Ross Thompson – UK

H) Jansher Khan – Pakistan

27

Name the women who hold the following world records

A) 200-metre sprint

B) 800 metres

C) 100-metre hurdles

D) 1 mile

E) High jump

F) Long jump

G) Javelin

H) Pole vault

28

What do the following pairs have in common?

A) Frank Ullrich and Fran Peter Rötsch

B) Barrie Jones and Keith Smith

C) Dawn Fraser and Krisztina Egerszegi

D) Marshall Jones Brook and Debbie Brill

E) Christy Ring and John Doyle

F) Bob Pratt and Peter Hudson

G) Mick the Miller and Patricia's Hope

H) Toni Sailer and Jean-Claude Killy

Land speed records

A) When was the land speed record set in a 4-wheel car?

B) What is this record?

C) What is the name of the car?

D) Who was the driver?

E) Where did it take place?

F) Which company made the engines?

G) What was the thrust of the car?

H) What other record was set?

Guess the sporting record-breaker

A) He worked as a ski instructor and bricklayer for eight years before he was strong enough for competition

B) He was only 25 years old in his second world cup season

C) He qualified for his first international competition in 1996

D) He won his first world cup race a month after breaking his hand, in 1997

E) He has, to date, won two gold medals

F) His preference is for racing giant slaloms, Super Gs, and downhills

G) He was the 1998 Overall World Cup Champion

H) He is nicknamed "The Herminator"

Name the nationality of the following record-holders

A) Joel Smets – Motocross champion

B) Kareem Abdul Jabbar – Basketball player

C) Paavo Nurmi – Athlete

D) Franz Klammer – Skier

E) Andre Ferreira – Equestrian

F) Michael Ferreira – Billiards

G) Stephen Roche – Cyclist

H) Welihinda Bennet – Cricket

Guess the year that the following occurred

A) Ilona Slupianek of East Germany shot put an Olympic best of 73ft 6.25in

B) Nadezhda Olizarenico was the Olympic record holder for the women's 800m at the end of the Games

C) Eric Heiden not only won all five men's speedskating events, but also set new records for each

D) Maurizio Damilano of Italy set a new Olympic record by walking 20km in 1 hour 23 minutes 35.5 seconds

E) In hammer throwing, Yuri Sedykh set a new world record with his 268ft 4in throw

F) The East German relay team ran the 4 x 100m in a world record time of 41.60 seconds

G) Vladimir Salnikov of the USSR made his country proud by winning the 1,500m freestyle in a world record time of 14 minutes 58.27 seconds

H) Rica Reinisch of East Germany set two new world records by winning the 100m and 200m backstroke events

33

Rugby World Cup

A) Which New Zealand player set the record for scoring the highest number of points in a single World Cup when he achieved 126 in the 1987 competition?

B) Which Scottish player scored a record 227 to be the highest points scorer after playing in the first three World Cups?

C) Name the English player who's the record try scorer with a total of 11 after the first three World Cups

D) Which country recorded the most points in a single game when they beat Singapore 164-13 in 1995?

E) Which French player became the first to score 30 points in a World Cup match, against Zimbabwe in 1987?

F) How many points did Simon Culhane of New Zealand score in 1995 to take the record for the highest scorer in a World Cup game?

G) Which team took the record for scoring the most tries in a single game with a total of 21 in a 1995 World Cup game?

H) Name the All Black who broke a record for appearing in 17 World Cup games

34

Indycar racing

A) Who set a record when he won the Indianapolis 500 from Scott Goodyear by 0.043 seconds, in the closest finish in Indycar history?

B) Who, in 1952, set the record for being the youngest Indy 500 champion, aged 22 years 2 months?

C) What unchallenged record was set in 1913 when Jules Goux beat Spencer Wishart by an incredible 13 minutes 8.40 seconds?

D) Who set a record in 1948 by becoming the only driver to win three consecutive Indycar World Championship titles?

E) Who won the Indianapolis 500 a record four times: 1970, 1971, 1978, 1987?

F) Who set a record by becoming the first black driver in Indycar racing?

G) Which Frenchman holds the record for being the first non-American to win the Indy 500 Championship title?

H) The best a rookie has done is come second in his first Indycar season. Who holds the record for being the first to achieve this?

What were the following the first to do?

A) Susan Brown

B) Trevor Francis

C) Adrian Moorhouse

D) Alfred Adolf Oerter

E) Cheng Jinlin

F) Manchester United

G) Giacomo Agnostini

H) Kurt Browning

Basketball

A) Which player is second to Michael Jordan as the highest NBA scorer?

B) Which national team claimed an unrivalled 11 gold medals in 13 Olympics when they won in 1996?

C) Which ABA player holds the record for being the only three-time scoring leader?

D) Who, in 1977, became the first woman to be selected in the NBA draft?

E) Which NBA team coach holds a record by leading his team to 1,189 victories in his 25-year career?

F) At the end of 1998, which team held the record for appearing in the most NBA finals?

G) Who was still hanging on to his record five-time win of the "Most Valuable Player" award at the close of the 1998 season?

H) Who holds the NBA record for scoring 840 free throws in a season?

37

Name the second sports in which the following record-holders also excel(led)

A) Fred Perry – Tennis player

B) Joe Davis – Snooker champion

C) Geoff Hurst – Soccer player

D) Johnny Weissmuller – Swimmer

E) Rob Andrew – Rugby Union player

F) Dennis Compton – Cricket star

G) Michael Jordan – Basketball player

H) Colin Jackson – Hurdler

38

Guess the sporting record-breaker

A) This team player is known for his consistent excellence over a very long career

B) He is the all-time career leader in passing accuracy (0.636), and has the highest quarterback rating (93.4)

C) In the 1991 and 1992 post-season runs, he threw 19 touchdown passes and no interceptions

D) He never completed less than almost 60% of his throws

E) From 1980 onwards, his quarterback rating per season remained at over 80

F) He was coached by the infamous Bill Walsh

G) He was rated "Most Valuable Player" in Superbowl XVI, XIX and XXIV

H) He played for the San Francisco 49ers

Record-breaking partnerships

A) Which female tennis partnership won a record eight successive grand slam doubles titles?

B) What is the highest partnership score in a Test Cricket match?

C) What is special about the winners of the 1992 Olympic Synchronised Swimming gold medal?

D) What nationality were the first tennis doubles pair to win all the grand slam events in one year?

E) Which rowing partnership has won two Olympic gold medals and three world titles?

F) Which horse and rider won the Women's World Championship Show Jumping twice?

G) Which pair completed the London Marathon tied together at the ankle and the wrist in a record time of 3 hours, 58 minutes and 33 seconds?

H) Which pair have won the amateur Eton Fives Championships 10 times?

40

The Grand National

A) Which horse has won the English Grand National a record three times?

B) Who was the first woman to complete the Aintree course?

C) Which record-breaking horse has won every other major English steeplechase but not won the National?

D) Who was the youngest jockey to win the Grand National?

E) Which horse has run the National a record eight times, winning twice?

F) Who was the first person to fall at Becher's Brook?

G) What is the fastest winning time?

H) What is the greatest amount of runners to participate in a Grand National?

41

Record-holding coaches, trainers and managers

A) Which horse trainer holds the record for the most career wins?

B) Who has both captained and managed a soccer world cup winning team?

C) Who has trained four Prix de l'Arc de Triomphe winners?

D) Which coach has made the most Super Bowl appearances?

E) Which horse trainer holds the record for most wins in the Belmont Stakes (New York)?

F) In which sport does the record-holding coach Daniel Topolski train?

G) Who coached Roger Bannister to success in the four-minute mile?

H) Who was Flo-Jo's manager?

42

Mount Everest

A) When was Mount Everest first successfully climbed?

B) Who accompanied Edmund Hillary on his trip to the summit?

C) Name the first woman to climb Everest

D) Who holds the record for the most Everest climbs?

E) Name the climber who was the first to complete the entire climb solo

F) How old was Ramon Blanco, the oldest climber to reach the top?

G) How tall is Everest?

H) What is the largest number of climbers to reach the summit in one day?

43

Guess the sporting record-breaker

A) He was considered to be one of his country's best soccer players by the time he was 17 years old

B) He is a left-footed player, who retired from the game on his 37th birthday

C) His most famous moment was when he dribbled the ball past ten English opponents from his own half, and scored

D) He scored a hat-trick against Lazio in his first season, leading Napoli to a 4-0 victory

E) He is recognised for leading Napoli to their winning of the 1988/89 UEFA Cup Final

F) He was disqualified in 1991 for testing positive for a banned substance, and went to play for Sevilla in Spain

G) He made his full international debut for Argentina in 1977

H) He was disqualified from the 1994 World Cup, again for the use of drugs, at the age of 34

44

Formula One

A) Whose record for the highest number of fastest average qualifying speeds remained unbeaten at the end of the 1998 season?

B) Who holds a record 51 race wins?

C) Which Formula One driver held the most World Drivers' Championship titles at the close of the 1998 season?

D) Which team has won a record nine Constructor's Championship titles?

E) Which circuit has held the most Grand Prix races between 1950 and 1998, with a total of 48?

F) Who set a Formula One record in 1972 for being the first two brothers to race Formula One at the same time?

G) Which driver set a record by winning four consecutive World Drivers' Championship titles from 1954-1957?

H) Who participated in a record 255 Grand Prix during his career?

45

Records you don't want

A) Which country hosted the 1976 Olympics but failed to win a single event?

B) Which athlete won 17 world records but never won an Olympic medal?

C) Which country holds the lowest Test Cricket score of 26?

D) Which soccer club has suffered the most consecutive losses?

E) Who failed to score a point in a 1982 Squash World Championship v Jahangir Khan?

F) Identify the boxer who was knocked down 14 times in a 1950 world title fight

G) Who holds the record for participating the longest in a cricket match without scoring?

H) Which two countries have hosted the World Cup but failed to reach the last eight?

46

Which sporting record-breaker said...?

A) "They performed better through the season and so they deserve the title"

B) "We're all given some sort of skill in life. Mine just happens to be beating up on people"

C) "It is necessary to relax your muscles when you can, relaxing your brain is fatal"

D) "Never let the fear of striking out get in your way"

E) "I don't know what I'm doing here. I can't sing, I can't dance, but just to be sociable I'll fight the best man in the house"

F) "Show me a millionaire with a bad backswing, and I can have a very pleasant afternoon"

G) "Half his game is 90 per cent mental"

H) "Experience is a great advantage. The problem is that once you get the experience, you're too damned old to do anything about it"

47

Flying

A) What was the first passenger plane to fly non-stop across the United States?

B) In what plane of under 1,000kg did Samuel Burgess of the USA reach an altitude of 3,000m in just 2 minutes and 18 seconds?

C) In what were Malcolm Ross and Victor Pather travelling in 1961 when they reached an unequalled height of 34,668m?

D) Which woman has equalled her own record eight times by flying for 15 hours and 11 minutes in a hot-air balloon?

E) In what flying machine have Paul Woessner and Coy Foster achieved a record speed of 77.50 k.p.h?

F) What is the claim to fame of "Glamorous Glennis", a Bell X-1 that flew in 1947?

G) In what did Pierre Allet achieve an altitude of 5,051m in 1996?

H) Who received a cheque for a whopping $25,000 in 1972 for flying from New York to Paris non-stop?

Wimbledon

A) Who was the first unseeded player to win the Men's Singles Final?

B) Which player has won the most Wimbledon titles?

C) Name the first player to win five consecutive Men's Singles Finals

D) Who was the youngest Women's Singles Champion?

E) Who was the first man to hold all four grand slam titles simultaneously?

F) What were Rod Laver and Neale Fraser the first to do in 1960?

G) Who made a record 36 appearances at the Championships?

H) Identify the oldest Wimbledon champion

49

Swimming

A) Who has won the most gold medals (7) in one Olympics?

B) Which swimmer became the world's youngest world record-holder in any sport in 1965 by breaking the 110-yard backstroke record in Blackpool, aged 12 years 10 months and 25 days?

C) Which female freestyle swimmer broke the 400m, 800m, and 1,500m Olympic and World Records in 1988/89?

D) Who, in 1875, was the first man to swim across the English Channel?

E) In 1981 who became the first man to achieve an English Channel triple?

F) Who holds the world record in the women's 50m breaststroke as of 1998?

G) Who was stabbed on returning home after Olympic success?

H) Who is the US swimmer who has equalled Mark Spitz' achievement by earning 11 Olympic medals to date?

Guess the sporting record-breaker

A) He holds a record over 72 holes of just 270 strokes

B) In the US Open he sliced his competition by a 12-point margin. That's a record for the tournament!

C) He broke three records in a single tournament in 1997

D) He was named "PGA Rookie of the Year" in 1996

E) He only turned professional in 1996

F) His first career win was the Las Vegas Invitational, which allowed him to play in the 1997 Masters

G) In 1997 he was the youngest winner of the US Open, taking the trophy at only 21 years of age

H) He was awarded "Athlete of the Year" in 1997, the first time in 26 years that it was won by a golfer

Which record-holders are hiding in the following anagrams?

A) Hail mud Mama (Boxing)

B) Given railing (Three-day eventing)

C) Race swill (Sprinting)

D) Nosy Rat Anne (Motor racing)

E) A bran liar (Cricket)

F) All sun Nelly G (Hurdles)

G) Get lost tripeg (Horse-racing)

H) Join lame chard (Basketball)

Golf

A) Who, in 1930, became the first golfer to win the Grand Slam?

B) Which father and son set records to become the oldest and youngest winners of the British Open respectively in successive years?

C) Which golfer can boast a record 18 titles - 6 US Masters, 4 US Opens, 3 British Opens, and 5 PGA Tours?

D) Which legendary golfer was the first to win four Masters?

E) Who, by the end of 1997, had notched up an unrivalled 88 wins in the Ladies PGA Championships?

F) Which PGA champion became the record individual earner in 1997 with nearly $12 million accrued?

G) Which two golfers share the record score of 272 for the US Open, set in 1980 and 1993 respectively?

H) Who, to date, has recorded the best score in the British Open?

Who was the first...?

A) Woman to sail across the Atlantic

B) Person to pick up a football and run with it, to launch the game of rugby football

C) Person to run the 100m in under 10 seconds

D) Person to reach the top of Mount Everest, in 1953

E) Lady player in the British Chess Championships to obtain a perfect 11-0 score

F) Westerner to attempt a bungee jump

G) High jumper to clear six feet using the then regulation feet-first technique

H) Woman to sail around the world non-stop, travelling 25,000 miles in 189 days

54

Guess the year that all the following occurred

A) The United States had collected a record 2,019 Olympic medals by this year, double that of its closest competitor

B) Steffi Graf was the world's number one in tennis for a record fourth consecutive time

C) The American women's 4 x 100m relay team set a record time of 41.47 seconds

D) Sebastian Coe's 16-year-old 800m world record was broken by the Kenyan Wilson Kipketer

E) Fred de Burghraeve set new Olympic and world records for the 100m breaststroke

F) Jan Ullrich set two new records in this year's Tour De France by averaging speeds of 24.38 m.p.h, and finishing 9 minutes and 9 seconds ahead of the person in second place

G) The new world record for pole vault was tied by Jean Galfione, Igor Trandenkov, and Andre Tpwontschik

H) Kerry Saxby-Junna set a new world record for the 5km walk by finishing in 20 minutes 13.26 seconds

55

Which is the odd one out and why?

A) Uruguay – 1930

B) Italy – 1934

C) Sweden – 1958

D) England – 1966

E) Brazil – 1970

F) West Germany – 1974

G) Argentina – 1978

H) France – 1998

56

Fishing

A) What is the weight of the largest recorded striped marlin caught on a fly?

B) What is the weight of the largest freshwater fish caught on a rod and reel?

C) What is the weight of the largest eel ever caught in Britain?

D) What record-sized fish did Randy Collins catch in Athens Lake, Texas, weighing just over 82Ib (37kg), in 1993?

E) Where was Adrian Bradshaw fishing when he caught an unbeaten near 214Ib (97kg) Nile perch?

F) What is on record as the largest seawater fish (non-mammalian) caught?

G) What fish at 9Ib 4oz, is the largest of its species ever caught?

H) What is the maximum weight allowed if a record-sized catch is to qualify for an IGFA All-tackle record?

The World Series

A) Which team has won the Series the most times?

B) Which player has made the most appearances in the World Series?

C) Which team has made the most appearances?

D) What is the record attendance for a single game?

E) Which pitcher has played in the most World Series?

F) Which player has had the most strikeouts?

G) Who is the only person to have scored a perfect game in the World Series?

H) Which player has had the most runs batted in 6?

Guess the country

A) This country is a seven-time winner of the tennis Federation Cup

B) The women's Triathlon World Championship has been won for the past three years by a woman from this country

C) It hosted the first Grand Prix of the 1998 Formula One series

D) It is the 20-time winner of the tennis Davis Cup

E) It won the 1988 women's field hockey Olympic title

F) It has won one single bronze medal for women's slalom

G) It was host of the eighth FINA Championship (aquatic sports), and came second in the medal list

H) It hosted the World Walking Championship in 1996, and the event was won by a local

Guess the sporting record-breaker

A) The NBA pickers blundered by selecting Sam Bowie ahead of him in his first season

B) He played his rookie season in 1984/85

C) His team have been NBA World Champions for five of the past seven seasons

D) He broke the points record held by Elgin Taylor of the LA Lakers by scoring 63 points in a game

E) He has 13 seasons of NBA experience, and has been named "Most Valuable Player" a record five times

F) He was selected for the NBA all-defensive first team a record ninth time in the 1997/98 season

G) He broke the NBA record in the 1997/98 season by scoring double-digits for the 788th consecutive game, robbing Kareem Abdul-Jabbar of the title

H) His career scoring average of 31.5 is the highest of any player in NBA/ABA history

Motorcycle racing

A) What make of motorcycle won the 500cc World Championship a record six out of eight times between 1962 and 1969?

B) Which FIM roadracing rider holds the record at the end of 1998 for an amazing 44 fastest race laps?

C) What was the first make of motorcycle to lap the Ulster Grand Prix course at over 100 m.p.h in 1939?

D) Who set a record by winning both the 350cc and 500cc Championship titles over five consecutive years?

E) What manufacturer became the first to win all the categories in the Manufacturers' Championships in 1958?

F) Who holds the record for having started in pole position in the most races?

G) Which rookie set a record by winning every race he finished in his amateur year in 1991, and turned professional at the end of that year?

H) Who beat Aaron Slight to snatch his record-breaking third World Superbike title?

61

Club and team records

A) Which soccer club has won the most league titles in Europe?

B) Which is the oldest golf club still in use?

C) The world's first yacht club was formed in 1720; what was it called?

D) Which American Football team has won the most NFL titles?

E) Which club has won the most Rugby League Challenge Cup Finals?

F) Which English soccer club has won the FA Cup the most times?

G) Which ice hockey team has scored the most games in one season?

H) Which baseball team has won the National League the most times?

What record-holders are hiding in the following anagrams?

A) LA stop rain (Motor racing)

B) Vain thing sags (Rugby)

C) Radical girl REM (Skiing)

D) Do Rainman (American Football)

E) Rave vest greed (Rowing)

F) Boast nice sea (Athletics)

G) When Jool (Darts)

H) Home corn Jen (Tennis)

63

Winter Olympics

A) Which speedskater set an incredible world record of 36.45 seconds in the 500m at the 1988 Summer Olympics?

B) At the close of the 1998 Winter Olympics, who retained her record high of six golds for speedskating?

C) Which ski-jumper became the youngest Olympic winner in 1992 at the age of 16?

D) Which alpine skier has won an unprecedented five Overall World Cup titles, but never an Olympic title?

E) Who held a record eight gold medals for cross-country skiing at the end of the 1998 Winter Olympics?

F) Which lady speedskater won an unmatched third consecutive Olympic gold medal with her Russian partner in 1980?

G) Which dominant Olympic ice hockey team have gone home victorious a record eight times?

H) Which doubles luge team slid to victory in a since unrivalled 1 minute 19.331 seconds in the 1980 Olympics?

Guess the year that all the following occurred

A) Joan Benoit of the USA set an Olympic record by winning the women's marathon in 2 hours 24 minutes 52 seconds

B) Daley Thompson of Great Britain took on the challenge of the decathlon and conquered it in an Olympic record time

C) The USA swimming team set three new world records in this year by winning the 4 x 100m and 4 x 200m freestyle events, as well as the 4 x 100m medley event

D) Carl Lewis won the 100m, 200m, and long jump, as well as anchoring the 4 x 100m relay team, to take two new world and Olympic records

E) Sebastian Coe set a new Olympic record time of 3 minutes 32.53 seconds in the 1,500m

F) In speedskating, Karin Ewke of East Germany set a new world record when she won the 1,500m event in 2 minutes 3.42 seconds

G) Carlos Lopes of Portugal set a new Olympic marathon record of 2 hours 9 minutes and 21 seconds

H) Tiffany Cohen of the USA set two new Olympic records when she won the 400m and 800m freestyle events

65

Cricket

A) Who holds the world record for the highest individual innings, with a total of 375, when the West Indies took on England in St. Johns during the 1994/95 season?

B) Which team won the 1996 World Cup by defeating Australia by a record seven wicket margin?

C) In which year was the first women's Cricket World Cup held?

D) Which "Wisden Cricketer of the Year" made his test debut against India in the 1991/92 season?

E) Which Indian cricketer teamed up with Vijay Merchant to set a test cricket record in 1936 for the most runs in a single day?

F) Which Sri Lankan player has made over 1,200 runs in test matches?

G) Which Pakistani player achieved dubious fame for breaking the arm of English captain Mike Brearley during play?

H) Which game in Colombo generated the highest total in the world during the 1997/98 season?

What do the following record-breakers have in common?

A) Terry Sawchuk – US

B) Abel Resino – Spain

C) Richard James Allen – India

D) Dino Zoff – Italy

E) Peter Shilton – England

F) Jacques Plante – Canada

G) Willie Fouke – England

H) Gerry Cheevers – US

Guess the sporting record-breaker

A) This player had the nickname "Blade"

B) He was an eight-time "Golden Glove" winner

C) He played for the Baltimore Orioles as shortstop

D) He won four pennants and the 1970 World Series Award

E) He had a career .977 fielding percentage

F) He is recognised as being instrumental in keeping players together through strikes in 1985, 1990, and 1994

G) He worked for the Baseball Players' Association after his retirement in 1982

H) He was ranked eighth all-time shortstop at the time of his death in 1998

68

Solutions

Page 1

A) The 7th hole at Satsuki Golf Course, Sanno, Japan - 881 metres long **B)** 20 lengths – Mayonnaise in the 1,000 Guineas, 1869 **C)** 5 hours, 26 minutes – Stefan Edberg and Michael Chang in the US Open semi-finals, September 1992 **D)** 40 years – Dr Ivan Osiier, Denmark, was an Olympic fencer between 1908 and 1948 **E)** "The Timeless Test" – South Africa v England, 3 –14th March 1939 **F)** 135.88 metres – Glen Edward Gorbous, 1st July 1957 **G)** 7 hours, 19 minutes or 110 rounds – Andy Bowen and Jack Burke in New Orleans in 1893 **H)** 204 metres (669ft) – Andreas Goldberger, Austria, 9th March 1996 in Harrachov, Czech Republic

Page 2

"Sugar" Ray Robinson

Page 3

A) 268.831 k.p.h. (167.044 m.p.h.) – Fred Rompelberg, 3rd October 1995 **B)** 241.448 k.p.h. (150.029 m.p.h.) – Jeffrey Hamilton, 14th February 1995 **C)** 46.52 knots (86.16 k.p.h.) – Yellow Pages Endeavour, Simon McKean and Tim Daddo, 26th October 1993 **D)** 69.62 k.p.h. (43.26 m.p.h.) – Big Racket – 5th Feb 1945, and Onion Roll, 1993 **E)** 67.32 k.p.h. (41.83 m.p.h.) – Star Title **F)** 44.631 k.p.h. (27.732 m.p.h.) – Alessio Gaggioli Radna, 7th September 1996 **G)** 43.35 k.p.h. (26.94 m.p.h.) – Carl Lewis and Ben Johnson, 1988 **H)** 8.64 k.p.h. (5.37 m.p.h.) – Tom Jager, 23rd March 1990

Page 4

A) The United States (7) **B)** The gymnast Louisa Semyonovna Latynina has won 18 medals **C)** Atlanta, 1996 (10,744 participants, representing 197 countries) **D)** Edward Patrick Francis Eagan, USA. He won the Light-heavyweight Boxing

Solutions

title in 1920 and was part of the US four-man Bobsleigh team in 1932 **E)** Oscar Swahan was aged 72 years and 280 days when he won a silver for shooting in 1920 **F)** Hubert Radaschal, Austria. A yachtsman, he competed in nine Olympic Games between 1964 and 1996 **G)** Marcel Depaille, who coxed the Dutch rowing pair to gold in 1900. He was believed to have been between seven and 10 years old **H)** Mark Spitz won seven gold medals for swimming in the 1972 Games in Munich

Page 5

1992

Page 6

A) 147 by Majed Abdullah of Saudi Arabia between 1978 and 1994 **B)** 30,427 people turned up at the Houston Astrodome to watch the "Battle of the Sexes" between Billy Jean King and Bobby Riggs, on 20th September 1973 **C)** 17. Prince Alexander Oblensky for the British team against Brazil in 1936 **D)** 16. By Stephan Stenis, of Racing Club de Lens, France, 1942 **E)** 215 – 33. Iraq v Yemen, New Delhi, November 1982 **F)** 219.83. Sweden, 1987. Aggregate 2,638 points from six games **G)** 301.70 m.p.h, by Kenny Bernstein in Budweiser King during qualifying at Gainesville, Florida on 20th March 1992 **H)** 86 – 2 in a "Friendly Army Tournament" between USSR and Afghanistan in Hungary, August 1981

Page 7

A) Brazil **B)** Antonio Carbajal, the Mexican goalkeeper, appeared in five World Cups between 1950 and 1966 **C)** Albert Roger Milla of Cameroon. He was 42 years and 39 days on 28th June 1994 **D)** Brazil **E)** Geoff Hurst (1966) **F)** Hungary scored 27 goals in five games during the 1954 World Cup **G)** Pele for Brazil **H)** 17 – 0. Iran beat the Maldives in a qualifying match on 2nd June 1997

Solutions

Page 8

Carl Lewis

Page 9

A) Juan Sebastian del Cano and crew, 1519-1522
B) Joshua Slocum (USA) 1895-1898 **C)** 74 days, 22 hours,
17 minutes, Sir Peter Blake and Sir Robin Knox-Johnston
D) Kay Cottlee (Australia) 1987/88 **E)** By helicopter
F) George Schilling, 1897–1904 **G)** 44 hours, 6 minutes,
David Springbett (UK) 1980 **H)** Steve Fossett

Page 10

A) W.G. Grace **B)** Bob Fitzsimmons: Middleweight 1891,
Heavyweight 1897 and Lightweight 1903 **C)** Althea Gibson
won the French Championship in 1956 and Wimbledon in
1957 **D)** Unre Hohn **E)** Dr Guiseppe Farina in 1950 in an
Alfa Romeo **F)** Stan Mellor. He rode 1,035 winners between
1952 and 1972 **G)** Roy Edwin Blowes, Canada, in 1987
H) Chris Evert

Page 11

A) Jack Nicklaus **B)** Tiger Woods **C)** Jack Nicklaus **D)** Ben
Hogan **E)** Craig Wood (1941, aged 39 years and four months)
F) Charles Kunckle **G)** Nick Price **H)** Jack Burke Jnr

Page 12

A) San Francisco 49ers and the Dallas Cowboys both have
won five times **B)** Charley Hayley **C)** The Dallas Cowboys v
the Pittsburgh Steelers at the XXX Super Bowl in 1996 was
watched by 138.5 million viewers in the US and 800 million
worldwide **D)** Joe Montana (3 times) **E)** 55 – 10 for the San
Francisco 49ers v the Denver Broncos in New Orleans, 1990
F) Chuck Noll (4 for the Pittsburgh Steelers)
G) The Pittsburgh Steelers v LA Rams in the XIV Super Bowl
at the Rose Bowl, Pasadena, in 1980 (103,985 spectators)

Solutions

H) The San Francisco 49ers v the San Diego Chargers, 49–26, in 1995

Page 13

America

Page 14

A) Saint–Denis, Paris. The Stade de France was built for the 1998 World Cup at a total cost of $466 million (£280 million) **B)** Stahov Stadium in Prague (240,000 spectators) **C)** The first ever FA Cup Final in 1923 (126,047 spectators) **D)** In Rio de Janeiro-Maracana Municipal Stadium (205,000 spectators) **E)** Denver, Colorado, USA. It is a mile above sea level **F)** Pontiac Silverdrome, home of the Detroit Lions **G)** Aztec Stadium, Mexico City **H)** Melbourne, Australia

Page 15

A) 11 years, 252 days **B)** 25 years **C)** 35 years **D)** 37 years **E)** 33 years **F)** 16 years **G)** 59 years **H)** 23 years

Page 16

Michael Schumacher

Page 17

A) USSR **B)** Switzerland (26) **C)** Australia in 1983 **D)** New Zealand v Japan: Score 145 – 17 in the Rugby World Cup in South Africa, 1995 **E)** USSR **F)** Hungary (6) **G)** USA **H)** Italy (5)

Page 18

1988

Page 19

A) Wilfred Bentitez, Puerto Rico, won WBA Light-welterweight aged 17 years 176 days, 6th March 1976 **B)** Michael Chang was 17 years and 109 days when he won the French Open in 1989 **C)** Jermaine O'Neale was 18 years

Solutions

and 53 days when he played for the Portland Trail Blazers, 5th December 1996 **D)** Coby Orr, USA, was five years old when he scored a hole-in-one in 1975 **E)** Emerson Fittipaldi, Brazil. 25 years 273 days, on 4th August 1957 **F)** Michal Martikan of Slovakia was 11 years old when he won the Whitewater slalom canoe event on July 27th 1996
G) Stephen Hendry. He was 21 years and 106 days on 29th April 1990 **H)** Voula Kouna, Greece. He was 9 years and 299 days in 1981

Page 20

A) Donovan Bailey, Canada, 1996, 9.84 seconds
B) Noureddine Morceli, Algeria, 1993, 3 minutes 44:39 seconds **C)** Colin Jackson, GB, 1993, 12.91 seconds
D) Javier Sotomayor, Cuba, 1993, 2.45 metres
E) Jonathan Edwards, GB, 1995, 18.29 metres
F) Jan Zelezny, Czech Republic, 1996, 98.48 metres
G) Jürgen Schult, GDR, 1986, 74.08 metres
H) Randy Barnes, USA, 1990, 23.12 metres

Page 21

A) Cricket **B)** Lacrosse **C)** Diving **D)** Hockey **E)** Marathon running **F)** Cycling **G)** Volleyball **H)** Darts

Page 22

A) 162.3 k.p.h (100.9 m.p.h) – Lynn Nolan Ryan for the Californian Angels in 1974 **B)** 10 seconds – Bart Brice, England, in a match against South Africa, 20th January 1923 **C)** 105.59 seconds by Keke Rosberg, Finland, in a Williams-Honda at Silverstone in 1995 **D)** 12 minutes 39.74 seconds – Daniel Komen, Kenya, on 22nd August 1997
E) 239.8 k.p.h. (149 m.p.h) by Greg Rusedski, 14th March 1998 **F)** 160.47 k.p.h. (99.7 m.p.h) by Jeffrey Thomson in the Australia v West Indies in 1975 **G)** 25 minutes 0.1 seconds – Grank-Peter Rötsch, GDR, in 1988

Solutions

H) 1 minute 27.30 seconds – Liv Hongyu, China, on 1st May 1995

Page 23

John McEnroe

Page 24

They all hold records for attaining perfect scores

A) The first person to pitch a perfect innings, 1880
B) He scored 10.0 in Compulsory Parallel Bars at the 1950 World Championships **C)** They hold the record for the highest tally of perfect sixes (29) at the World Ice Dance Championships, Ottawa 1984 **D)** He was the first snooker player to record the maximum break of 147 – Griffiths, New South Wales, 1934 **E)** He was the first diver to be awarded the perfect score of 10.0 by all 7 judges, in the US Olympic Trials, 1972 **F)** She was the first gymnast to score a perfect score at the Olympic Games, when she scored seven 10.0s at Montréal, 1976 **G)** He won all seven races on the race card at Ascot 28th September 1996 **H)** She won the 1988 Olympic title having received perfect scores in all six disciplines

Page 25

A) Joe Davis **B)** Stephen Hendry (21yrs) **C)** Make two maximum breaks (147) **D)** John Higgins **E)** Steve Davis
F) Ronnie O'Sullivan **G)** John Parrott **H)** John Higgins

Page 26

A) $13.1 million **B)** JR's Ripper had 143 wins between 1982 and 1986 **C)** Hauso, ridden by Capt. Alberto Larriguiber Morales, jumped 2.47 metres in Chile, 5th February 1949
D) 32,318 km (20,081 miles) **E)** Ballyregan Bob (32)
F) A Great White shark at 1,208.38 kg by Alfred Dean, Australia 21st April 1959 **G)** Cigar **H)** JJ Doc Richard, 63 in 1995

Solutions

Page 27

A) Eton fives **B)** Badminton **C)** Racketball **D)** Real tennis
E) Tennis **F)** Table tennis **G)** Rackets **H)** Squash

Page 28

A) Florence Griffith Joyner, USA, 1988, 21:34 secs
B) Jarmila Kratochvilova, Czech Republic, 1983, 1 min 53:28
secs **C)** Yordanka Donkova, Bulgaria, 1988, 12:21 secs
D) Svetlana Masterkova, Russia, 1996, 4 mins 12:67 secs
E) Stefka Kostadinova, Bulgaria, 1987, 2.09 m **F)** Galina
Chistyakova, USSR, 1988, 7.52 m **G)** Petra Felke, GDR,
1988, 80.00 m **H)** Emma George, Australia, 1998, 4.59 m

Page 29

A) Both won the Biathlon World Cup twice **B)** Both scored a
soccer goal in a record six seconds **C)** They are the only
swimmers to have won their Olympic event on three occasions
D) The first man and woman to have cleared a 6 foot high
jump **E)** They both won the All-Ireland Hurling
Championships a record eight times **F)** They are the only
Australian Rules Footballers to have scored 150 goals in a
season **G)** They are the only dogs to have won the English
Greyhound Derby twice **H)** They were the first two skiers
to complete the Olympic treble of slalom, giant slalom
and downhill

Page 30

A) October 1997 **B)** 1,227.985 k.p.h. (763.035 m.p.h.)
C) The Thrust SSC **D)** Andy Green **E)** Black Rock Desert,
Nevada **F)** Rolls-Royce **G)** 50,000lb **H)** It was the first car
to break the sound barrier

Page 31

Hermann Maier

Solutions

Page 32
   A) Belgian **B)** American **C)** Finnish **D)** Austrian
   E) South African **F)** Indian **G)** Irish **H)** Sri Lankan

Page 33
   1980

Page 34
   A) Grant Fox **B)** Gavin Hastings **C)** Rory Underwood
   D) Hong Kong **E)** Didier Camberabero **F)** 45 **G)** New
   Zealand **H)** Sean Fitzpatrick

Page 35
   A) Al Unser Jnr **B)** Troy Ruttman **C)** Widest margin of
   victory ever **D)** Ted Horn **E)** Al Unser Snr **F)** Willy T Ribbs
   G) Jules Goux, in 1913 **H)** George Amick, in 1958

Page 36
   A) She was the first woman to take part in the Oxford and
   Cambridge Boat Race **B)** He was the first English soccer
   player to be sold for £1 million **C)** He was the first swimmer
   to swim 100 metres breaststroke in less than a minute
   D) He was the first person to win four consecutive Olympic
   titles in the same event (Discus) **E)** She was the first female
   weightlifter to clear lift more than twice her body weight
   (90kg) **F)** They were the first English club to win the League
   and FA Cup double twice **G)** He was the first motorcyclist to
   win both 350cc and 500cc world titles for five consecutive
   years (1968–72) **H)** He was the first skater to achieve a
   quadruple jump in competition

Page 37
   A) Glen Rice **B)** USA **C)** Julius Erving **D)** Lucy Harris
   E) Lenny Wilkens **F)** LA Lakers, 24 finals
   G) Kareem Abdul-Jabbar **H)** "Mr Clutch" Jerry West

Solutions

Page 38

A) Table tennis **B)** Billiards **C)** Cricket **D)** Water polo
E) Cricket **F)** Soccer **G)** Baseball **H)** Long jump

Page 39

Joe Montana

Page 40

A) Pam Shriver and Martina Navratilova **B)** 567 by Sanath
Jayasuriya and Roshan Mahanama in the India v Sri Lanka
1997/98 Test **C)** They are identical twins **D)** Australian –
Frank Allan Sedgeman and Kenneth Bruce McGregor won the
US Open, Wimbledon, the French Championship and the
Australian Championship in 1951 **E)** Steve Redgrave and
Matthew Pinsent **F)** Janou Tissot and Rocket in 1970 and
1974 **G)** Dale Lyons and David Pettifer in 1995
H) Brian Matthews and John Reynolds

Page 41

A) Red Rum (1973, 1974, 1977) **B)** Geraldine Rees, riding
Cheers in 1982 **C)** Desert Orchid **D)** Bruce Hobbs was 17
years old when he won on Battleship in 1938
E) Manifesto **F)** Captain Becher **G)** 8 minutes 47.8 seconds
– Mr Frisk, 1990 **H)** 66, 22nd March 1929

Page 42

A) Dale Bard (USA) had 7,200 winners between 1962 and
1996 **B)** Franz Beckenbauer. He captained the West German
team to victory in 1974 and managed the West German
champions in 1990 **C)** Andre Fabre **D)** Don Shula. He won
five victories for the Miami Dolphins and one for the
Baltimore Colts **E)** James Rowe Snr (8) – 1883–84, 1901,
1904, 1907–08, 1910, 1913 **F)** Rowing – he coached the
Oxford Boat Race team to a record 10 successive victories
from 1976 to 1985 **G)** Franz Stampfl, the Oxford University

Solutions

Coach **H)** Her husband, the athlete Al Joyner

Page 43

A) 29th May 1953 **B)** Sherpa Tenzing Norgay (Nepal)
C) Junko Tabei (Japan) **D)** Ang Rita Sherpa (Nepal)
E) Reinhold Messner (Italy) on 20th August 1980
F) 60 years and 160 days on 7th October 1993
G) 8,848 metres (29,029 feet) **H)** 40 on 16th May 1993

Page 44

Diego Maradona

Page 45

A) Nigel Mansell **B)** Alain Prost **C)** Juan-Manuel Fangio (5)
D) Ferrari **E)** Monte Carlo **F)** Emerson and Wilson Fittipaldi
G) Juan-Manuel Fangio **H)** Riccardo Patrese

Page 46

A) Canada **B)** Ron Clarke **C)** New Zealand **D)** Stockport
County FC lost 39 League and Cup games between 1976 and
1978 **E)** Maqsood Ahmed in the ISPA Championship Final
F) Danny O'Sullivan (UK) in a Bantamweight fight against Vic
Towel (SA) **G)** Godfrey Evans (England) played for 97
minutes – Australia v England, Adelaide, 1947
H) Spain (1982) and the United States (1994)

Page 47

A) Michael Schumacher **B)** "Sugar" Ray Leonard
C) Stirling Moss **D)** Babe Ruth **E)** Rocky Marciano
F) George Low **G)** Yogi Berra **H)** Jimmy Connors

Page 48

A) DC-7 **B)** Bucker Jungmeister **C)** A free balloon
D) Jetta Schantz **E)** An airship **F)** First plane faster than speed
of sound **G)** Backpack-powered microlight **H)** Charles
Lindbergh

Solutions

Page 49

A) Boris Becker **B)** Billy Jean King won 20 titles **C)** Bjorn Borg, 1976 – 80 **D)** Lottie Dodd, 15 years 285 days, 1887 **E)** John Budge, 1938 **F)** They played the first left-handed final **G)** Arthur Gore between 1888 and 1927 **H)** Margaret Evelyn Du Pont, 44 years and 125 days when she won the Mixed Doubles with Neale Fraser

Page 50

A) Mark Spitz **B)** Karen Muir **C)** Janet Evans **D)** Matthew Webb **E)** Jon Eriksen **F)** Penny Heyns **G)** Alexander Popov **H)** Carl Osburn

Page 51

Tiger Woods

Page 52

A) Muhammad Ali **B)** Virginia Leng **C)** Carl Lewis **D)** Ayrton Senna **E)** Brian Lara **F)** Sally Gunnell **G)** Lester Piggott **H)** Michael Jordan

Page 53

A) Bobby Jones **B)** Tom Morris Snr & Jnr **C)** Jack Nicklaus **D)** Arnold Palmer **E)** Kathy Whitworth **F)** Greg Norman **G)** Jack Nicklaus & Lee Janzen **H)** Greg Norman

Page 54

A) Anne Davison, 1952–53 **B)** William Webb Ellis **C)** Jim Hines, 9.95 seconds, 1968 **D)** Sir Edmund Hillary **E)** Miss E. Tramner **F)** Kal Muller, 1970 **G)** Marshall Brooks **H)** Kay Cottee

Page 55

1996

Page 56

Brazil – 1970

Solutions

All the other countries played in the Soccer World Cup Final when it was hosted in their countries. Barring Sweden, the other six also won the Final as host nations

Page 57

A) 212lb (96kg) **B)** 468 lb (212kg) sturgeon **C)** 24lb (11kg) (Britain) **D)** Smallmouth Buffalo **E)** Lake Nasser, Egypt **F)** 2,664lb (1208 kg) great white shark **G)** American eel **H)** 130 lb (59kg)

Page 58

A) The New York Yankees have won 24 times **B)** Lawrence "Yogi" Berra has played 14 times **C)** The New York Yankees (35 appearances) **D)** 92,706 – Los Angeles Dodgers v Chicago White Sox (5th game) at Memorial Coliseum, Los Angeles, 6th October 1959 **E)** Whitey Ford (11 appearances) **F)** Robert Gibson (17) 2nd October 1968 **G)** Donald Jones Lawson, 8th October 1956 **H)** Robert C. Richardson, 8th October 1960

Page 59

Australia

Page 60

Michael Jordan

Page 61

A) Suzuki **B)** Mick Doohan **C)** 495cc AJS V4 **D)** Giacomo Aggostini **E)** MV Augusta **F)** Mick Doohan **G)** Colin Edwards **H)** Carl Fogarty

Page 62

A) Glasgow Rangers have won the Scottish League 47 times **B)** Gentlemen Golfers, established in 1744, was renamed the Honourable Club of Edinburgh Golfers. The Royal and Ancient of St Andrews is 10 years younger **C)** Water Club of Cork, Ireland **D)** Green Bay Packers (11 times)

Solutions

E) Wigan (16 times) **F)** Manchester United (nine times)
G) The Detroit Red Wings (62 games in the 1995/96 season)
H) LA Dodgers (19 times)

Page 63

A) Alain Prost **B)** Gavin Hastings **C)** Marc Girardelli
D) Dan Marino **E)** Steve Redgrave **F)** Sebastian Coe
G) John Lowe **H)** John McEnroe

Page 64

A) Uwe–Jens Mey (East Germany) **B)** Lydia Skoblikova
C) Tony Nieminen (Finland) **D)** Marc Girardelli **E)** Bjorn
Dahlie (Norway) **F)** Irina Rodnina **G)** Soviet Union/Russian
teams **H)** East Germany

Page 65

1984

Page 66

A) Brian Lara **B)** Sri Lanka **C)** 1978 **D)** Shane Warne
E) Mushtaq Ali **F)** Chandika Hathurusingha **G)** Sikander
Bakht **H)** Sri Lanka v India

Page 67

They all hold records as goalkeepers
A) He played a record 971 games as an ice hockey goalkeeper
B) This soccer goalie prevented a goal being scored for a
record 1,275 minutes **C)** This hockey goalkeeper conceded
no goals in the 1928 Olympics **D)** He holds the soccer
goalkeeping record for international matches, 1,142 minutes,
without conceding a goal **E)** He made a record 1,280 senior
British appearances **F)** This ice hockey goalkeeper has a
record 434 NHL wins **G)** He is the heaviest soccer goalie
H) This ice hockey goalkeeper went a record 32 games
without defeat

Page 68

Mark Belanger